stargazer's kitchen

Synecdoche
Joshua Kurtz, Editor
Kimberly Meilun, Editor

stargazer's kitchen

poems by William Hicks
art by Maggie Hazen

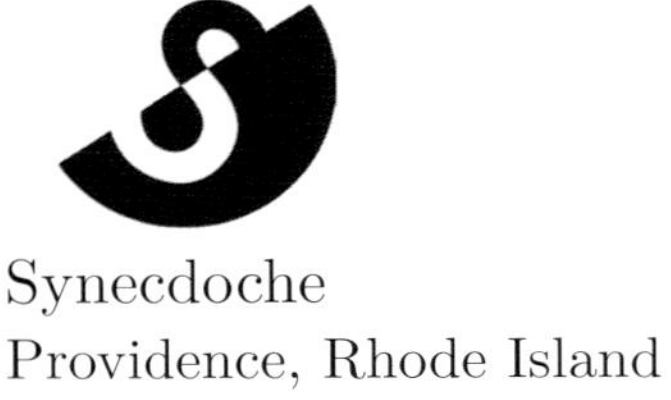

Synecdoche
Providence, Rhode Island

Published by Synecdoche Press, Providence, RI, 02912
Text copyright © 2015, William Hicks
Visual art copyright © 2015, Maggie Hazen
ISBN: 978-0-9963677-0-7

Manufactured in the United States of America

for Loren Baker

and

for Clifford B. and Rachel Hicks
with love and gratitude

midwinter

  mailboxes afloat
    on snowdrift
 and us naked
   in the window

 our laughter
   pours sap
  into willows

shakes snowskirts
 from pine trees
    to match
 our [forest's] nakedness

  the world so cold
my nipples
  stand on end
 even behind
    glass

 but if we
   declare it spring
 who would not
follow us?

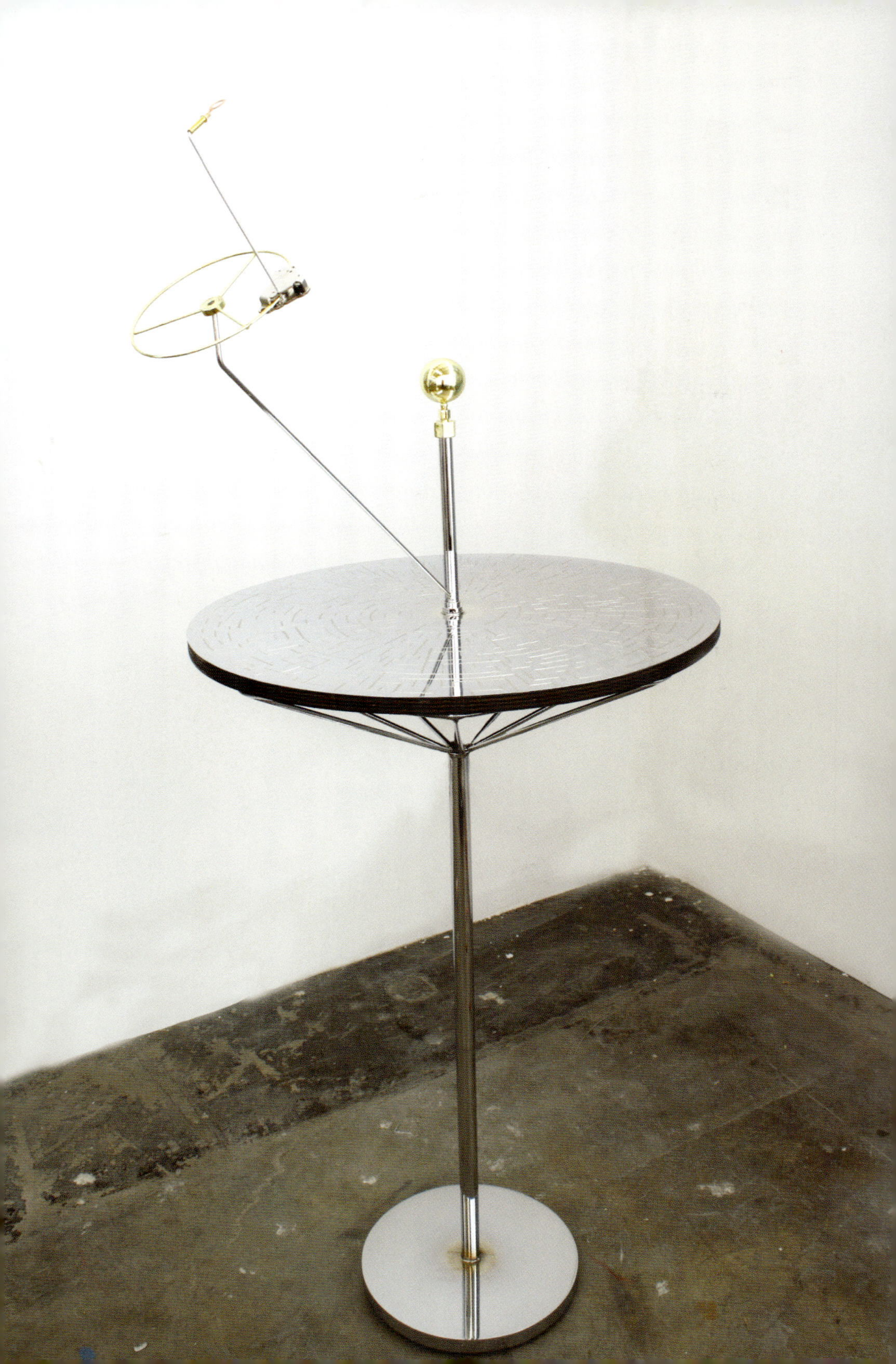

perseids

stepping on a moonlight grating
dust grinds at stairs
beneath furtive feet

briars trip into notice
tugging at her socks as the girl
turns to watch the clouds

in an airy cup
of all the wrong shape
she sees her streak

even bending upward eyes
find nothing that can be told
and so she watches

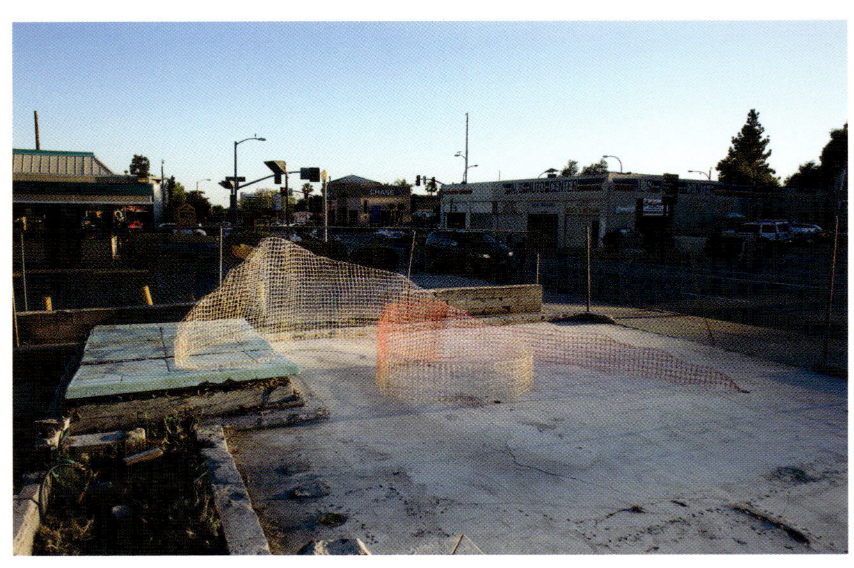

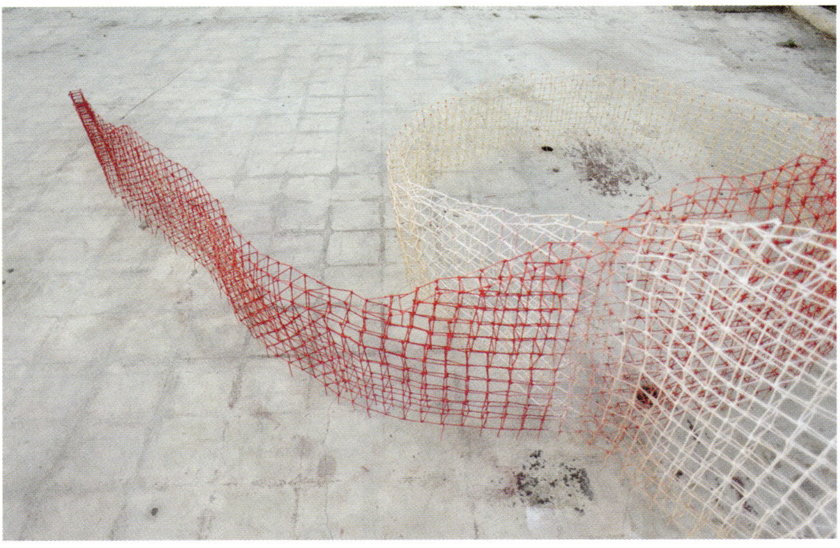

titmouse

when we found it
   on low thin branches
you offered to climb for it
   and I was jealous
for the first time

but father said
   don't touch the eggs
and so we stared instead
   and walked around it
rubbing our knuckles on
   paper-bark

maybe she felt it
and left them
there with shells
glowing through
gathered twigs

maybe she
   returned with
worried singing

*sometimes you must look
away from the sun to see
the rainbow in goose down
falling from abandoned
branches*

but we saw nothing
  and wandered back
for lunch catching
  baggy clothes
  on catbriar

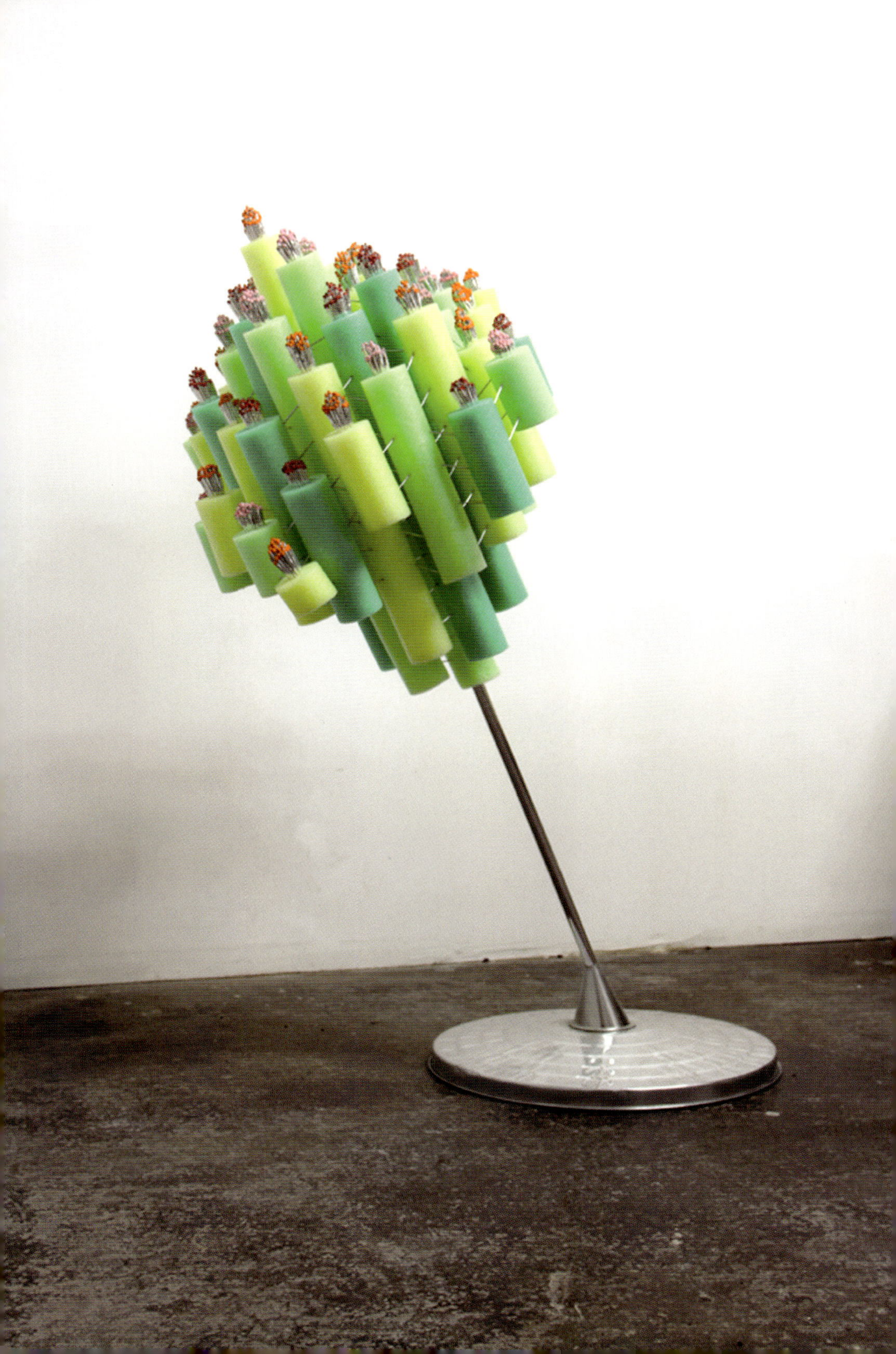

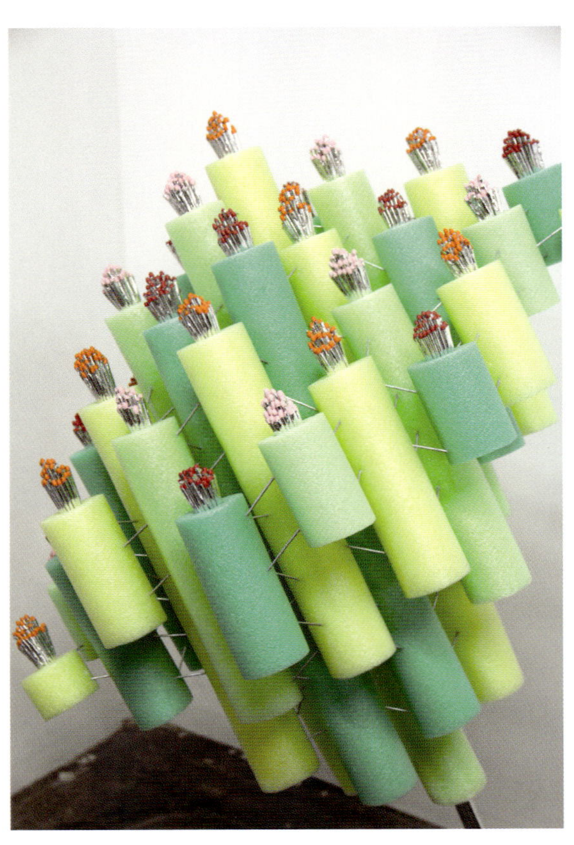

sanibel

knee-deep in
waves she
waits for
sunset
camera
clutched above
salt spray

behind her
other feet
press sand
other ears
press gulls

she is first to turn west

clouds absorb
sunbleed
and now
the beach in
rush-hour hush

she waits

firedrop flattened
        by water's edge
     it catches in
quiet shutters
     turns sails into
shadows

she waits

the sun beneath
    the water now
she feels the beach
        emptying–

            the others
                on ticktime
            can't conceive
        of a brightening

purple turns
    to darker blue

and then
    jewel-weed
blossom

        she's moving again
runs up and down
        the beach
pushes sand into
        toeprints
            camera clicking

                and

        she walks home
            with rising
tide

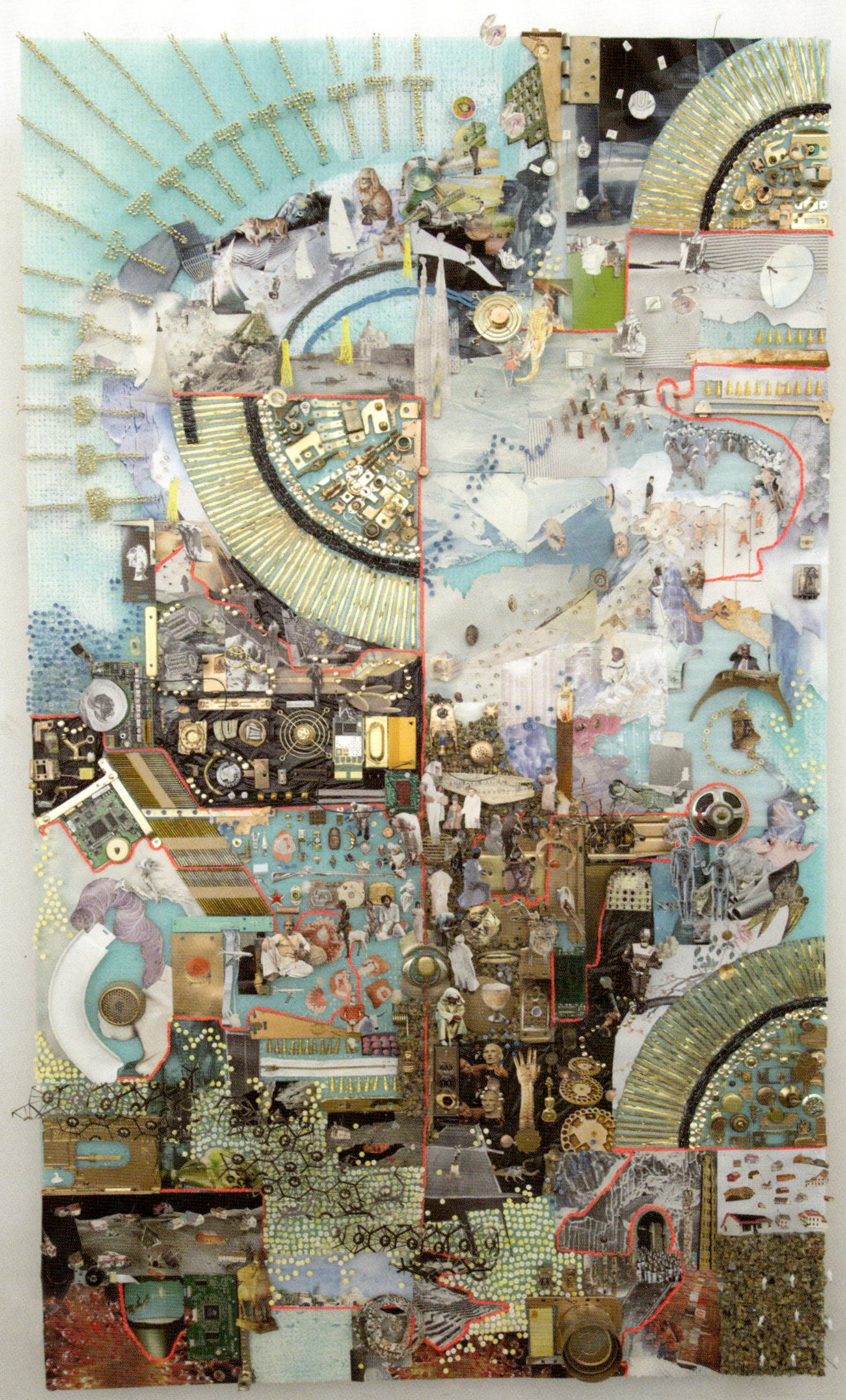

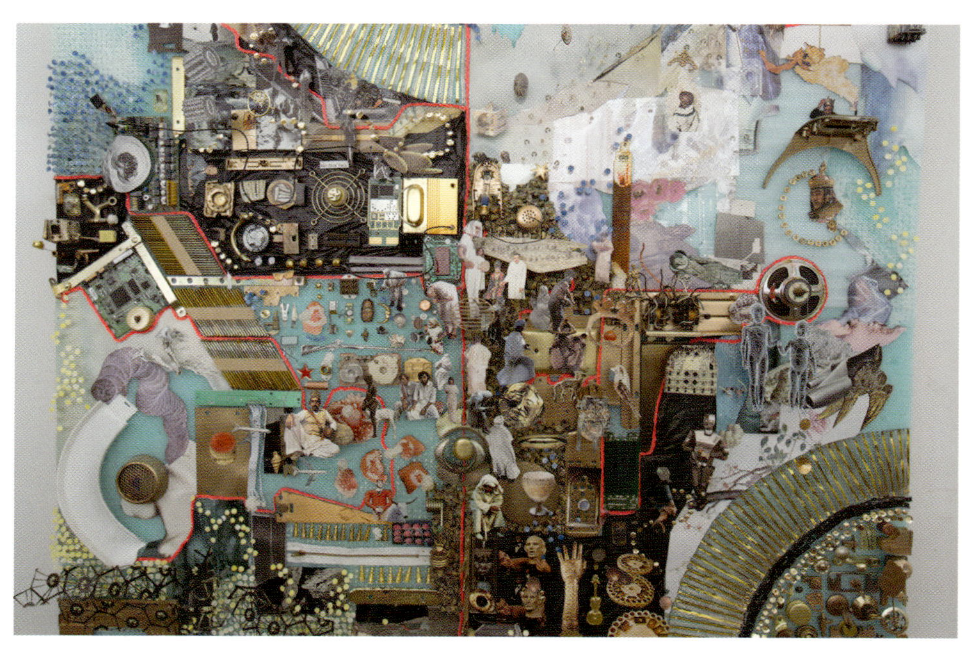

attic room

straddling a chair
   she writes backwards
 in the margins
     of St. Augustine

    tears out pages
       into a scroll
   with scotchtape

    lets it splash in
      to her lap
     mix with a flowerprint
            skirt

  even in september
     it's too hot
  up here to
  wear anything
      but flowerprint

she stands up
   walks around herself
   paces like piccaso tigers

there's enouph tapping in
      her fingertips to smooth
   what cloathes she wears

                  enouph writing in the
                     scroll to
                        wrap her slender waste

fruit flies by
      the rockingchair
   she bought too many
                     aapplles
      can't bear to
   throw them out

      she feels bad about
                        that
         feels bad about
                        her attic room
            hangs a Cézanne over
               paintcracks
         to cheer the place up

                           it works marvelously

she sits
        down again
    writes the
        aapplles in
                to St. Augustine

keeps
going

    writes new
        print in
            to her skirt

keeps
going

    writes new
        paint in
            to her walls

sun
rise

    wraps her
        slender waste

    falls herself
            in to
                        corner
            bed

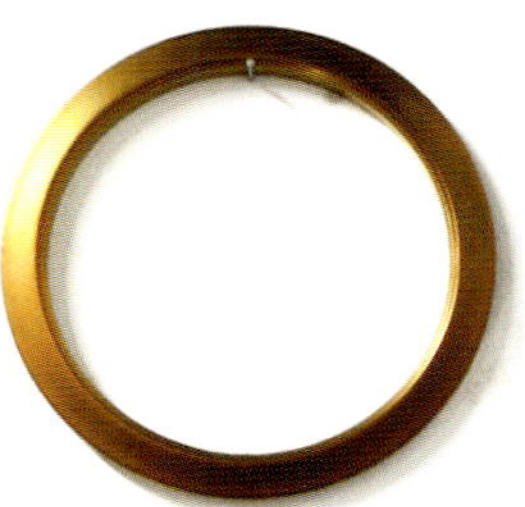

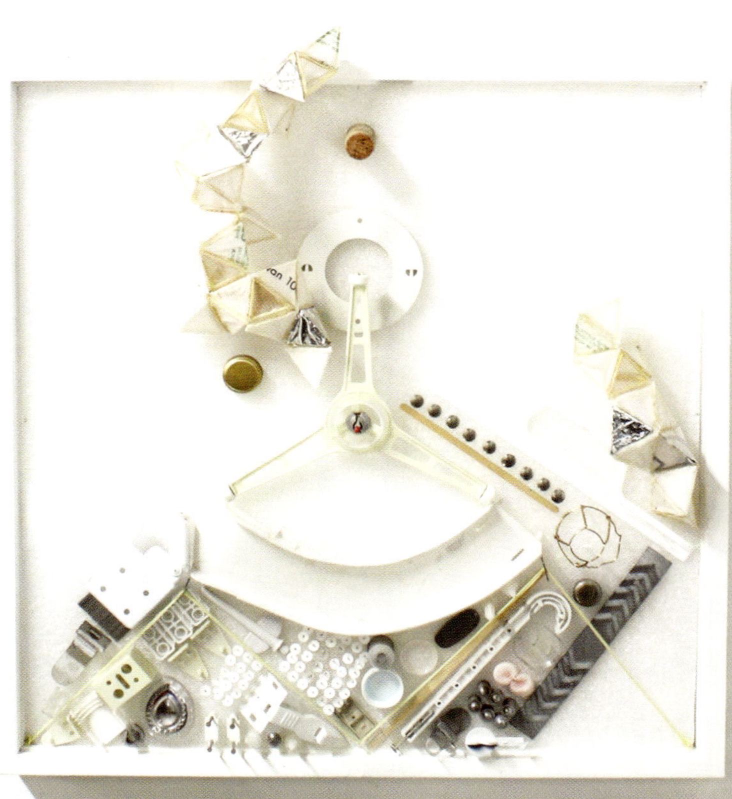

inspired

with

each   blueness

unraveled   word   of   her

thought   spread   in   ink   whispers   winding   outward   scattered

on   distant   dinner   tables   pages   unmarked   revealing   missed   charcoal   strokes   or   touches   moving   slowly   toward   conclusions

sailors   memory   rings   hollow   waits   cools   settling   calm   doubt   clamoring   rises   stops   chaos   crumbled   meaning   fades   marks   bends   swaying   mind   ducking   straight   toward   risk   stillness   envelopes   moves   touching   houses   that   remain   quiet

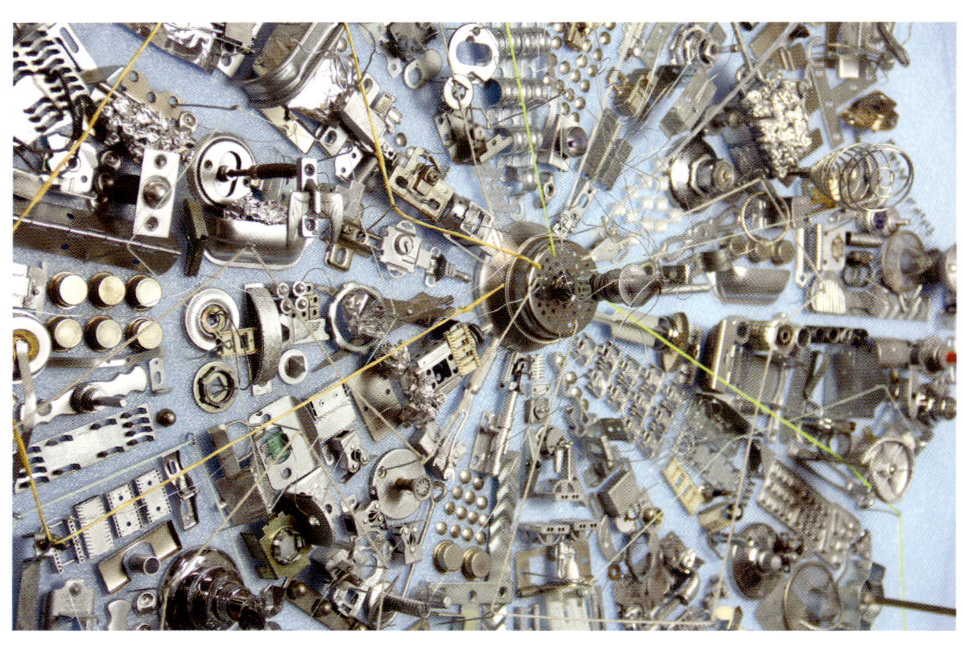

account

packing our summer into boxes
i run out of tape
    just keep going
          throw torn scraps
of paper on top

shopping lists
receipts
a budget we made
but never followed
    everything we'll
never need again
    dumped into cardboard
scraped thin from
          other moves

pressed leaf you saved
from a picnic
swimsuit broken
in the straps
notebook full of
dates and tallies

that summer you
        cooked sausages
        by the Kinderhook
    and i counted
        greyhound buses
    without you ever knowing

listened for them
        grinding over the bridge
stepped out of
        razor-cold water
    to mark them every time

                    if i told you now
                  you would say you
              didn't believe me
                                find schedules
        to check my work
                but we aren't wading
          anymore
                    no clearing by
        the changing-bridge
              no stream
          veneered on
        rocks to slice
                    our feet
        and my notes
                    already buried
                    under half-
        started scrapbooks

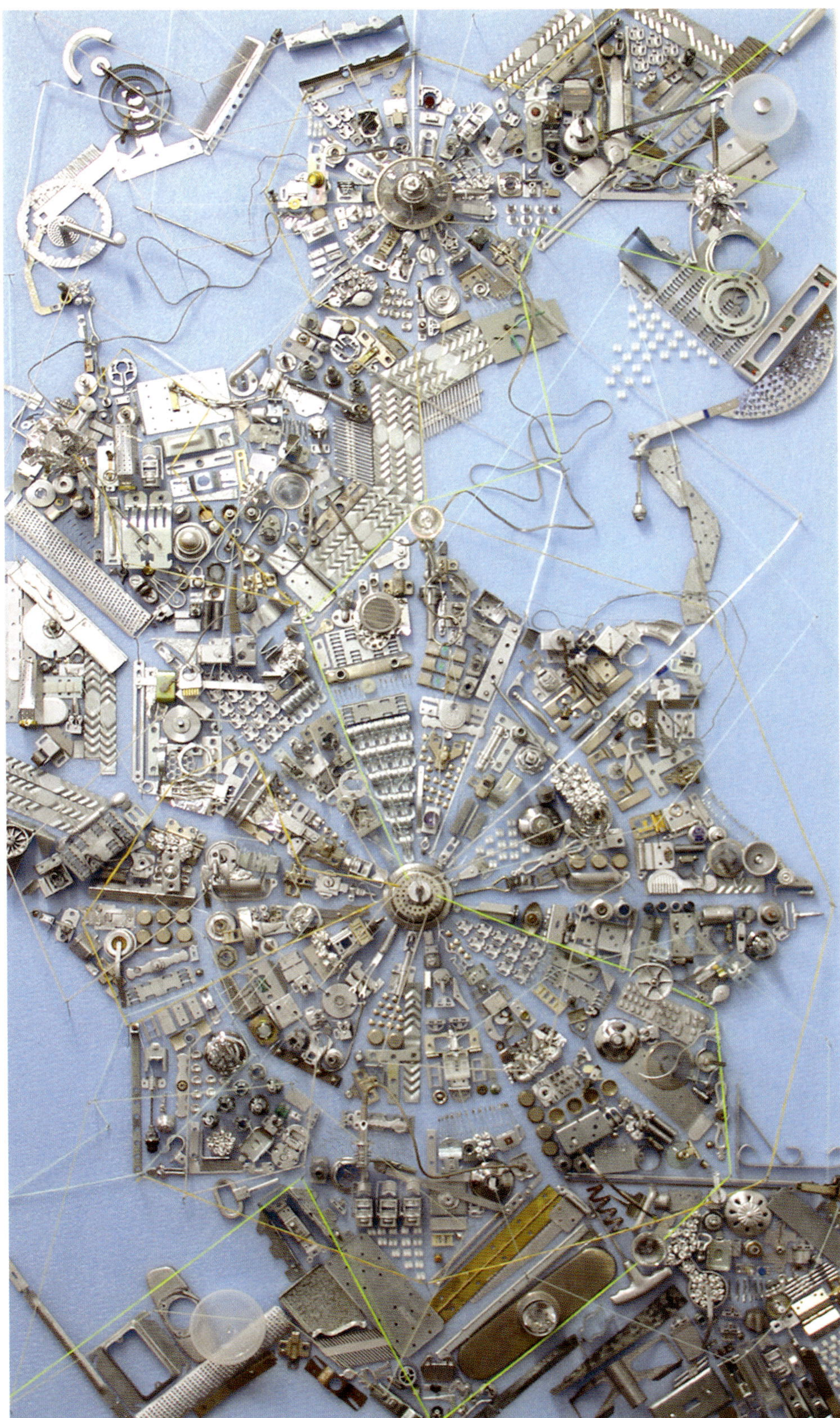

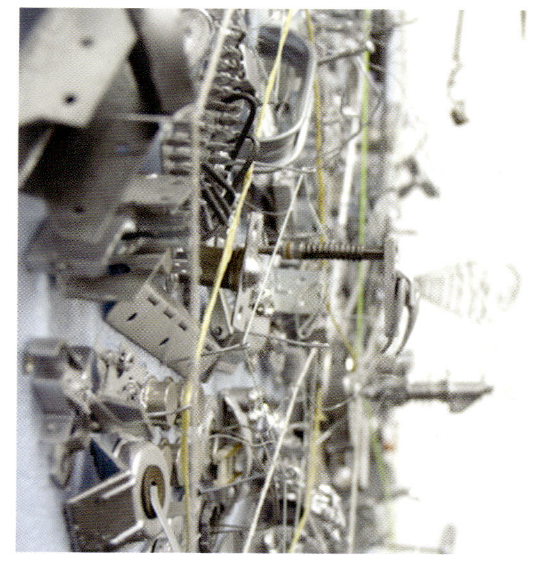

moon cellar

        headlights on
            a rusty shopping
    cart dragged through town

    one wheel stuck
        scratching slate
      at twilight
            he limps along

            old man with
    his cart full of moons
        muttering to himself
      spit running
                down his beard
        inventory too precious
    to sell

*phobos deimos ganymede metis io adrastea europa
amalthea callisto thebe mimas enceladus tethys dione
rhea titan iapetus (my strange child, never did
understand him the way i should) hyperion janus helene
triton naiad nereid...*

this is the man
	with the tides
  in his palms
	lamps glowing
silverdust
	drooling
  icicles

looks up through clouds
	shaking off
headlight dazzle
	never should have sold that one
	never did name it proper
	such sweet light

*deimos phobos metis ananke proteus titania (her face
cracked and smoothed and cracked again) ariel thalassa
atlas leda elara thebe ananke prometheus carme callirhoe
themisto himalia calypso tarvos ymir pan...*

he makes his way
        home
    sets the door back
in place
        lifts rotting
floorboards to
    lay his work
underneath

staring upwards
        he stays awake
till dawn
    watches every planet
leak through
            the ceiling

phobos deimos io metis...

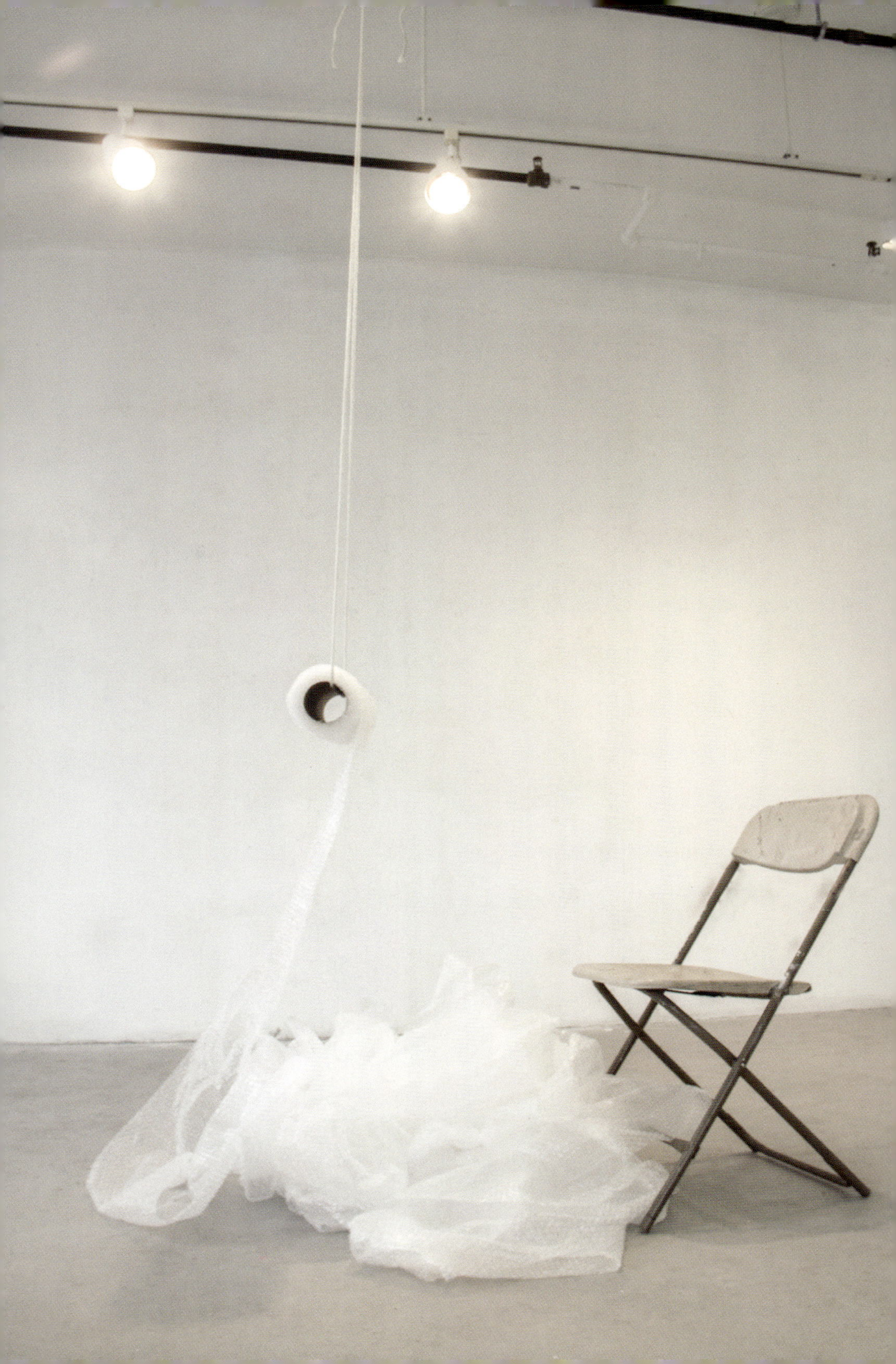

birds out of inkjars

familiar words sung

in a foreign hotel room

birds out of inkjars

familiar words sung

in a foreign hotel room

clash with the carpet

birds out of inkjars collapse

back into blotted paper

                        familiar words sung
                          in a foreign hotel room
                            clash with the carpet

        unwashed blankets
          and in the drip of the faucet
            familiar words sung

                            while i write postcards
                              birds out of inkjars collapse,
                                clash with the carpet
            i can't tune it out
              hear my own name in every
                familiar word sung
                                        as they ring through pipes
                                          hidden by dirty paintings,
                                            clash with the carpet
                        back into blotted paper
                          familiar words sung
                            clash with the carpet

I
familiar words sung can become
strange, draw barstool jokes
into opera halls, turn sex
into lovemaking

II
changing clothes in a foreign hotel room
you never worry who is watching
they will never see you again

III
a boy staying overnight
in a stranger's house
drops a dirty red t-shirt
on the bed
just to clash with the carpet

IV
her crying:
loud enough to scare
birds out of inkjars, collapse
mud into bricks

V
startled,
even a warship will
back into blotted paper

familiar

room:
carpet

unwashed blankets
and   the drip of
words

while ı wrıte

ınkjars collapse,

ı can't
hear my own name
sung

through pıpes
hidden   paıntıngs,

blotted paper

words   become

clothes in a

                    stranger's

                         bed,

                              collapse
              into

       startled

                              paper

familiar

wash
                of
        words

                                collapse

                                        through

                                        paper

b

l

r

d

s

overwritten

                two of us writing on this
        page—it's a mercy you're left-
        handed

                clicking
                    into inkrun

                    there's going to be a
        reckoning soon

                we entered into this knowing
        the risks but not the outcome and
        now   teetering over blank
        pages

                every squabble
                    preserved
                    in

        your breathing,
                your voice:
            birds out of inkjars

                    scrolls
                        into pages
            into scrolling

        we are out of type—

                and it was always going to end

        in apostrophic plurals

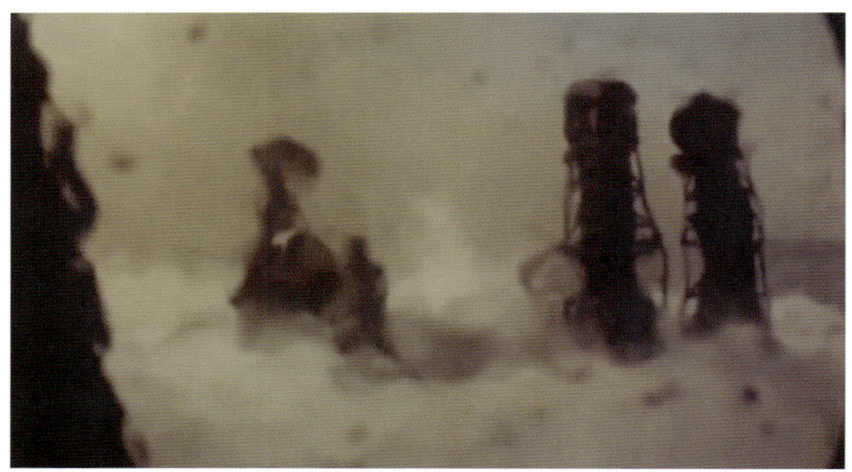

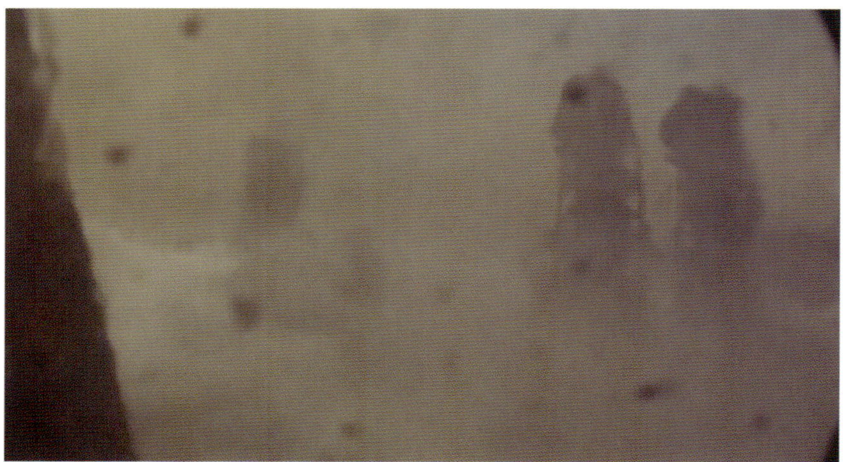

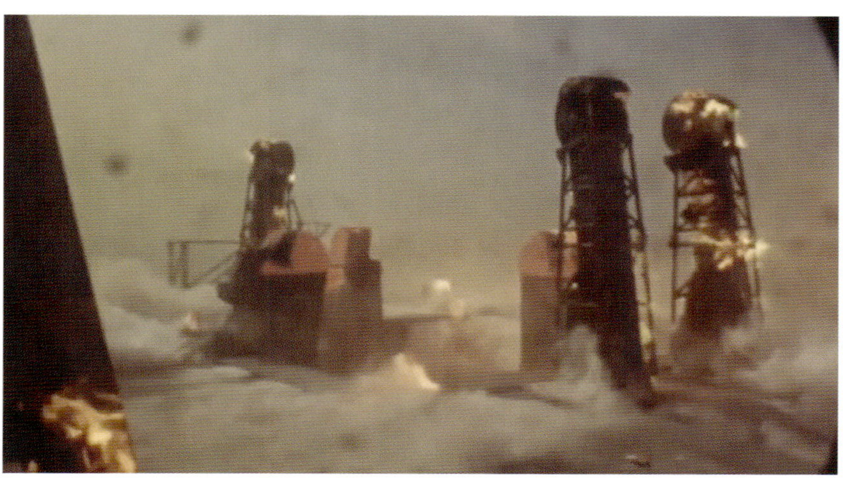

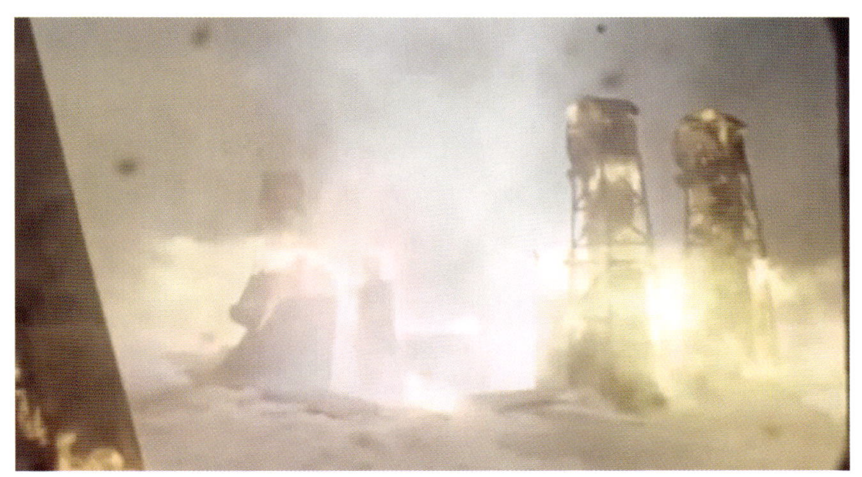

sparrowcross

above my grandmother's mantle—
    two stuffed sparrows, their wings
      spread out and dipped in wax
    mounted beak to beak—
a macabre cross

    each year at christmas trying
not to stare at them, knowing
    not to ask about them

    i know how to keep a silence

know how to protect it from
  barbarian hordes: never
let them know its value
    bury it in ashpiles, empty lots
  not churches and libraries

i showed my silence
     to someone once—
digging it out from
          rows of thigh-high corn
  in a neighbor's field
      for a girl i thought i loved

   it had been buried
so long
     she brushed right past it

pulled me down
          beneath the corn

one year i burned
those sparrows:

  fireplace cremation and
feigned confusion
    christmas day—

          saving
      my silence
         for the ashes

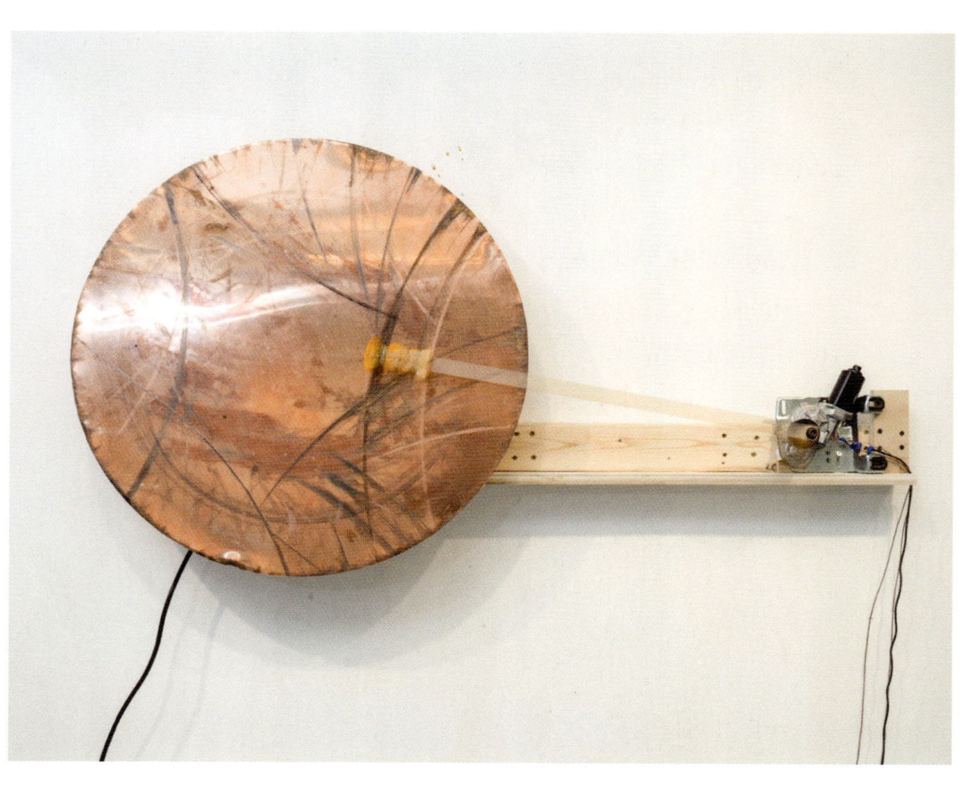

4:53 to boston

red house repetition of
     a train line blurs
a hundred hidden smiles
   in newly-planted gardens
to a thought of rail noise
     and moving boxes

our grey rush can't strip
   moss from broken walls
can't drag color through
     expectant stones
but shakes teacups in
     polished sinks

inside sleepers nod with
each uneven tie
foreheads sliding against
clean glass drifting
toward strange wakings

with dawn we watch
    a truck roll
beside us in unplanted fields
    leave it behind
turn to papers and forgotten
    breakfast

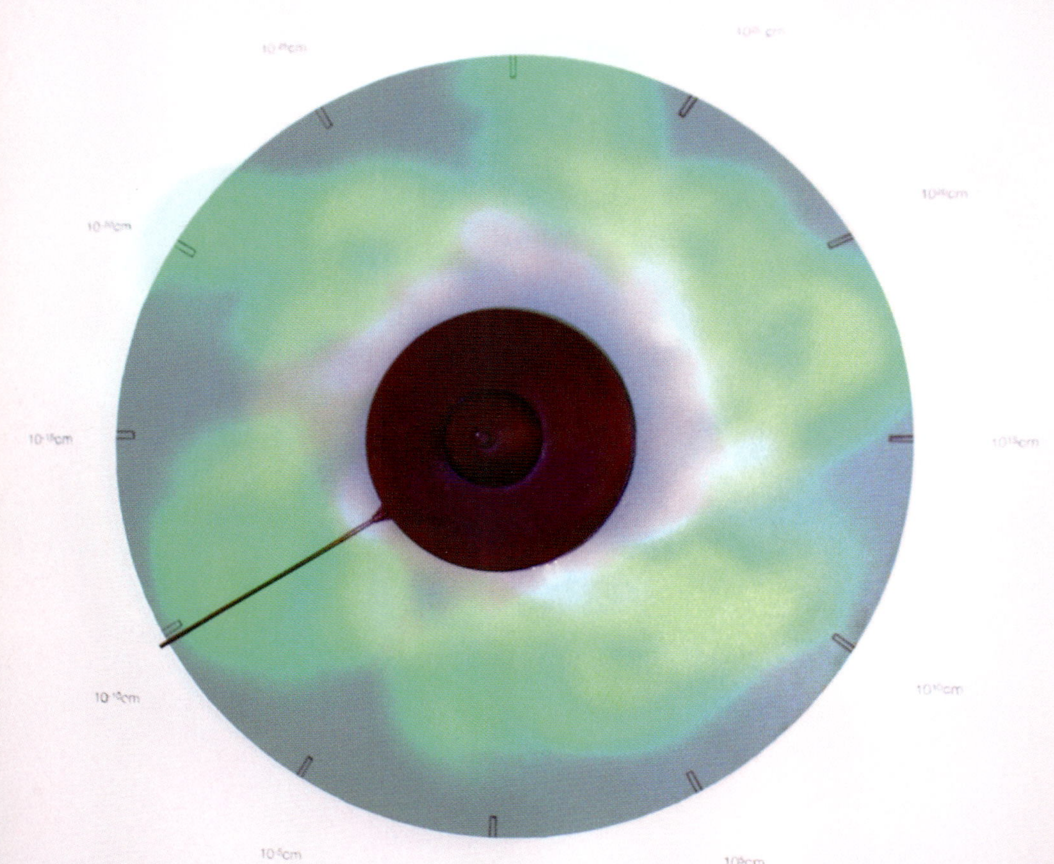

1cm
10⁻⁵cm
10⁵cm

dinner party

cooking pork chops
      in august
  she burns one side,
isn't sure whether
  to serve them
  dark side up

standing by the grill
  she
    daydreams
  of forest fires

firefighters
  keeping "in the black–"
what would they do?

what would emily post do

in a forest fire?

a forest can't
burn twice
but pork chops can

she gives up
brings them inside
slips sideways through
a sliding glass door
haloed in pigsmoke

waterfalled
laughter
and she's
through dinner
sweeps her guests   *won't you let us help with the dishes*
out the door   *marvelous must do this again*
                         no really it was delicious
                         must send me all the recipes

cars starting
at the base of the driveway
leave her
quiet

she moves from
        room to room
          cleaning up
        pieces of her guests
             lips left on wineglasses
             feet on the sofa
                  perfume everywhere
      sweeps it all into
white garbage bags
        blows out every shadow

in the kitchen
        she stacks
                oversized plates

                builds soapsud
towers

        waits for collapse

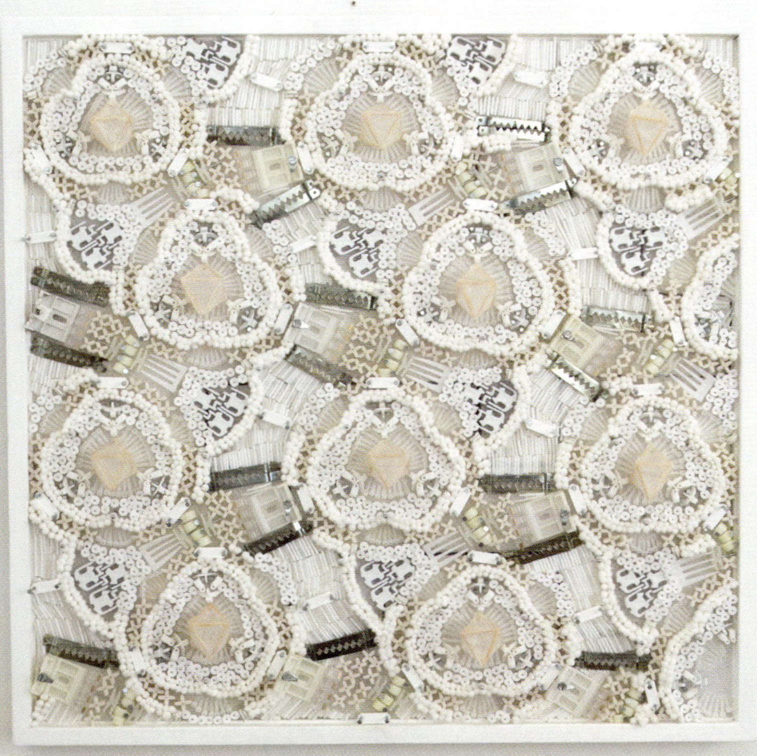

11:35

altered upon minor dilemma
her fingers nervously push
pleated cloth flat and tap
behind a faint settled sob

in the hush of a dark taxi
remembered faces haunt her
caught in a smell of lilac
kissing toward wasted silk

she looking through drapes
disrobes for warm imagined
lovers and wakes beautiful
there beside offered fruit

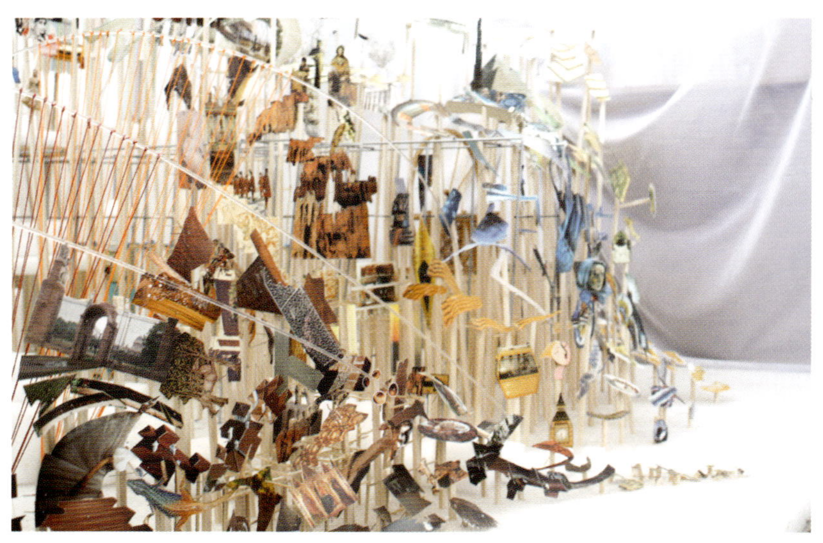

grasping times

an assurance wakens her

that damp scent
    within the sky
provided her
        visionless desire

spots may streak
  her
      frontier place
  that lanes
  a solitary meadow

she will live
among
   still saplings
and bob
from fresh dirt edge
   to present fold
and load a swing
   built with
     cedar
     scraps

   her paths
will not yet see
       edges
pressed from
     orange blossoms

inside her
            sky
she
       builds
              a
        spot

she
   rests
        alone
for a time

and walks back
   through
     waist-high
   grass

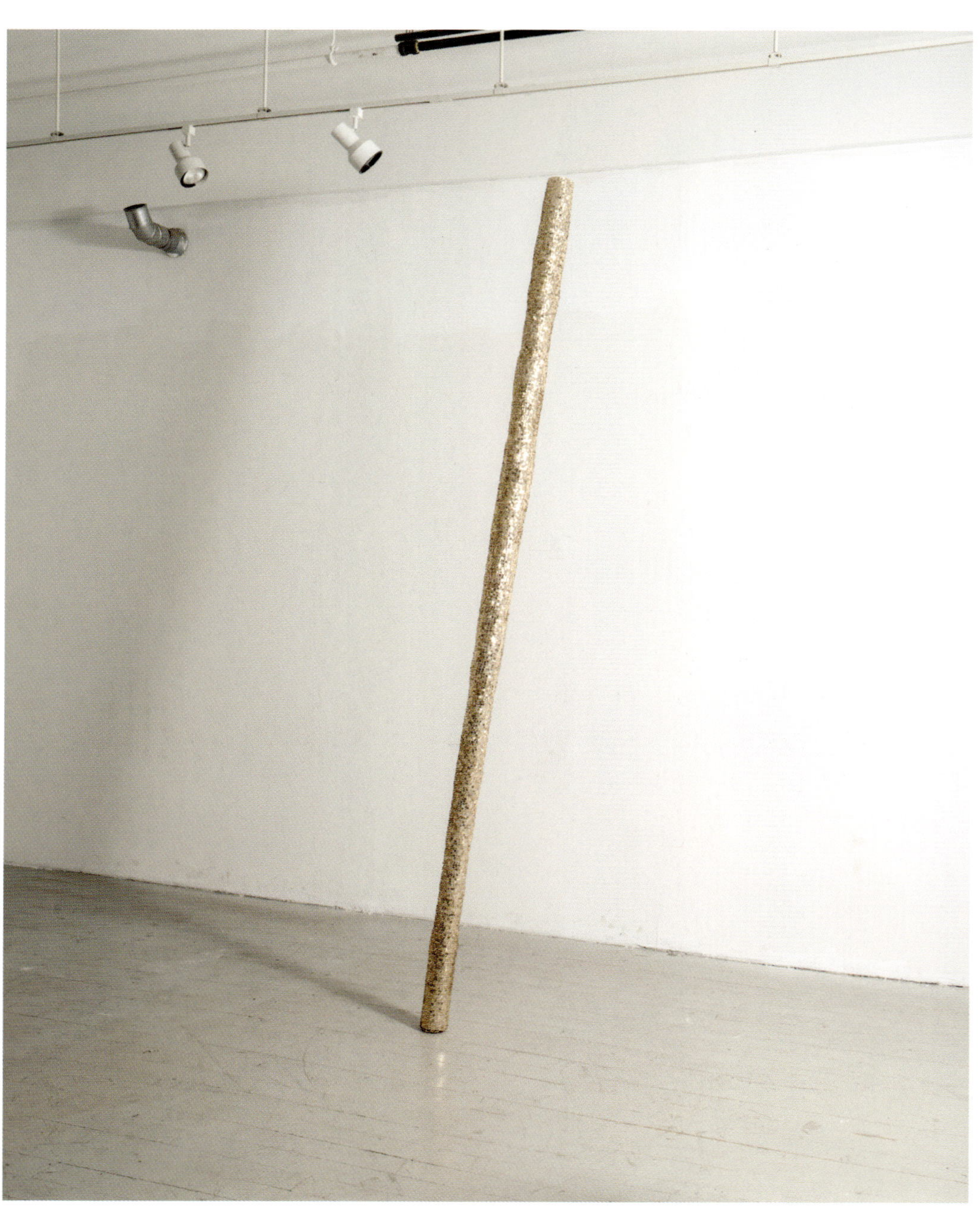

blackrock

driving back down blackrock mountain the storm's still going
and both of us soaking wet shivering the rain out of t-shirts
plastered on like wall-paper you complain how hair this long
is awful when it's wet and I've got the good sense not to tell
you you look beautiful—thunderstorm gathered up in every
strand—but I tell you anyway you're asleep already though
knotted up under a towel and still shivering and I watch the
wipers peel away water from a turn where the valley opens
up past a guardrail

riverline

the rain's picking up and I can hardly see the bark on the
trees if you were awake you'd be watching for other cars but
there is no one and we drive on sloshing the asphalt into
water-ribbons down mountain curves i'm not sure where
we're going you always figure out hotels

rainmirror

we hit the bottom of the valley turn onto another road and there's a car zipping water into spray it's gone and i turn the other way going anywhere away from other people going down along the river protecting our silence and just like that it's over light coming through in a ray like it's not real life like somebody painted it pointing down where the road climbs again ripping through our blanket-fort clouds sunquiet

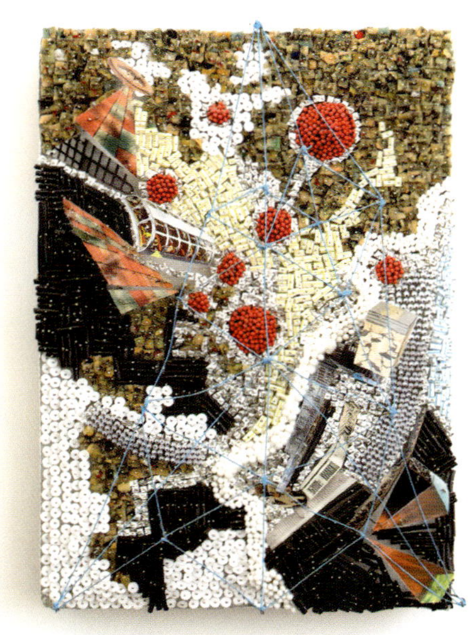

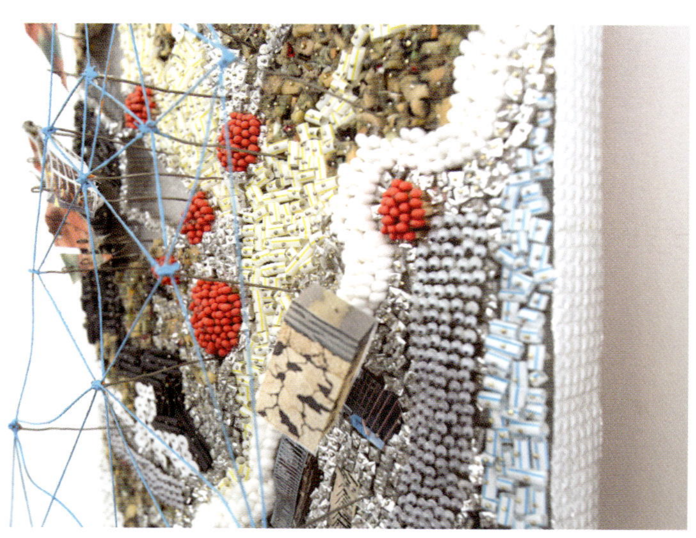

transit

their living room found
   a joy in allowed
   between
      fingers
   behind
      curtains and doors
and sheets tacked over
    ground-floor windows

   his belt scrapes
on clean
   floorboards
climbing out of bed
    at dawn

reaching at a doorknob
    her hand touches
  a damp robe
    turned rough
  with soap stains

crumbled leaves wander
    on a welcome mat
  beside two pairs
    of mud-streaked shoes

in the kitchen
    he strings socks
  over mixing bowls
and dangles
  dripping sleeves
in glasses

laughter breaks a
  watching
turns lamps
  into sunbeams
on papered
        walls

with evening
        he turns on
        shadows
    paces by leaves
    in pots

as she brushes her
    hair

he looks through
    open doors
and leans
    against a
chipped shelf

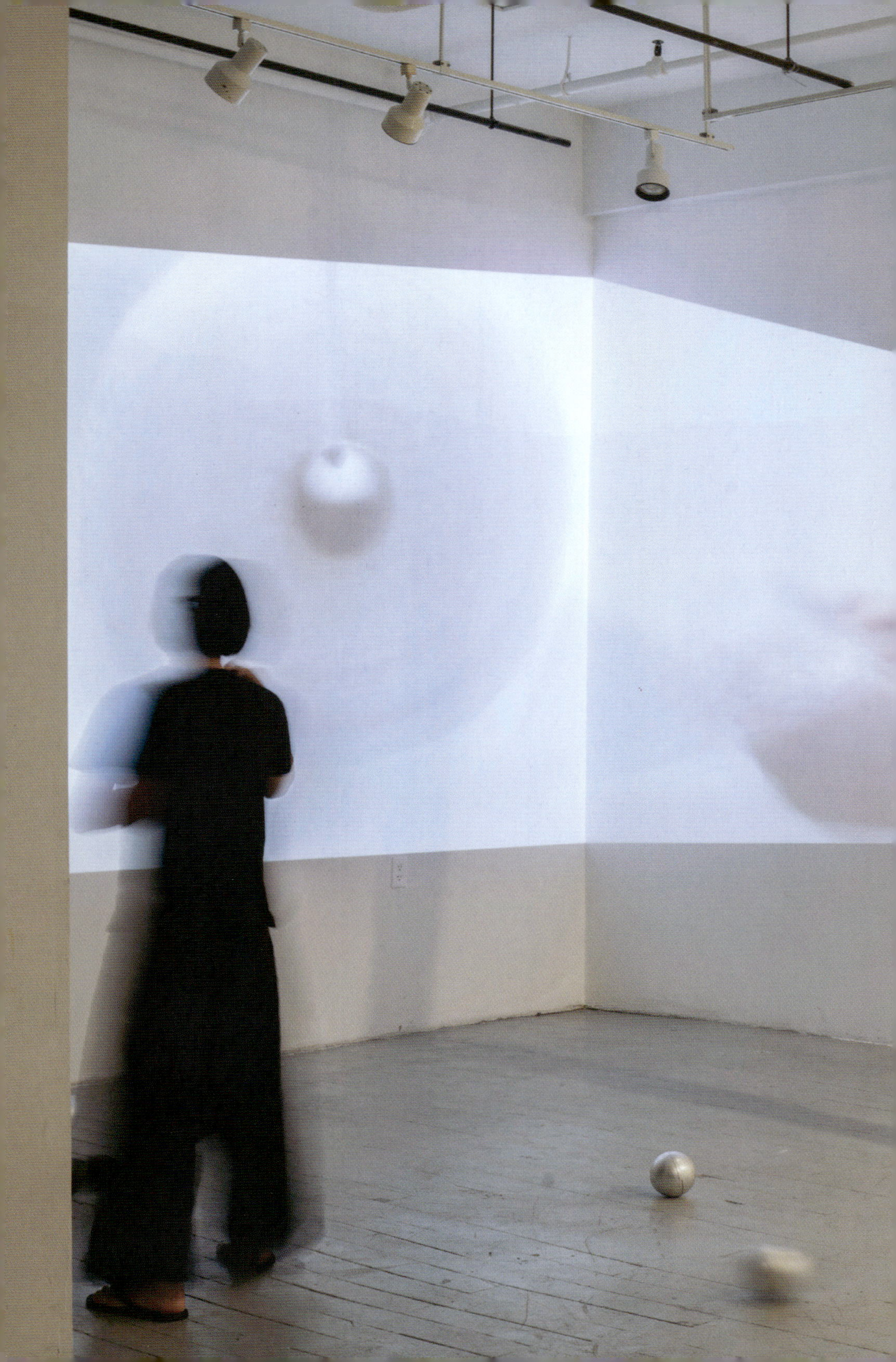

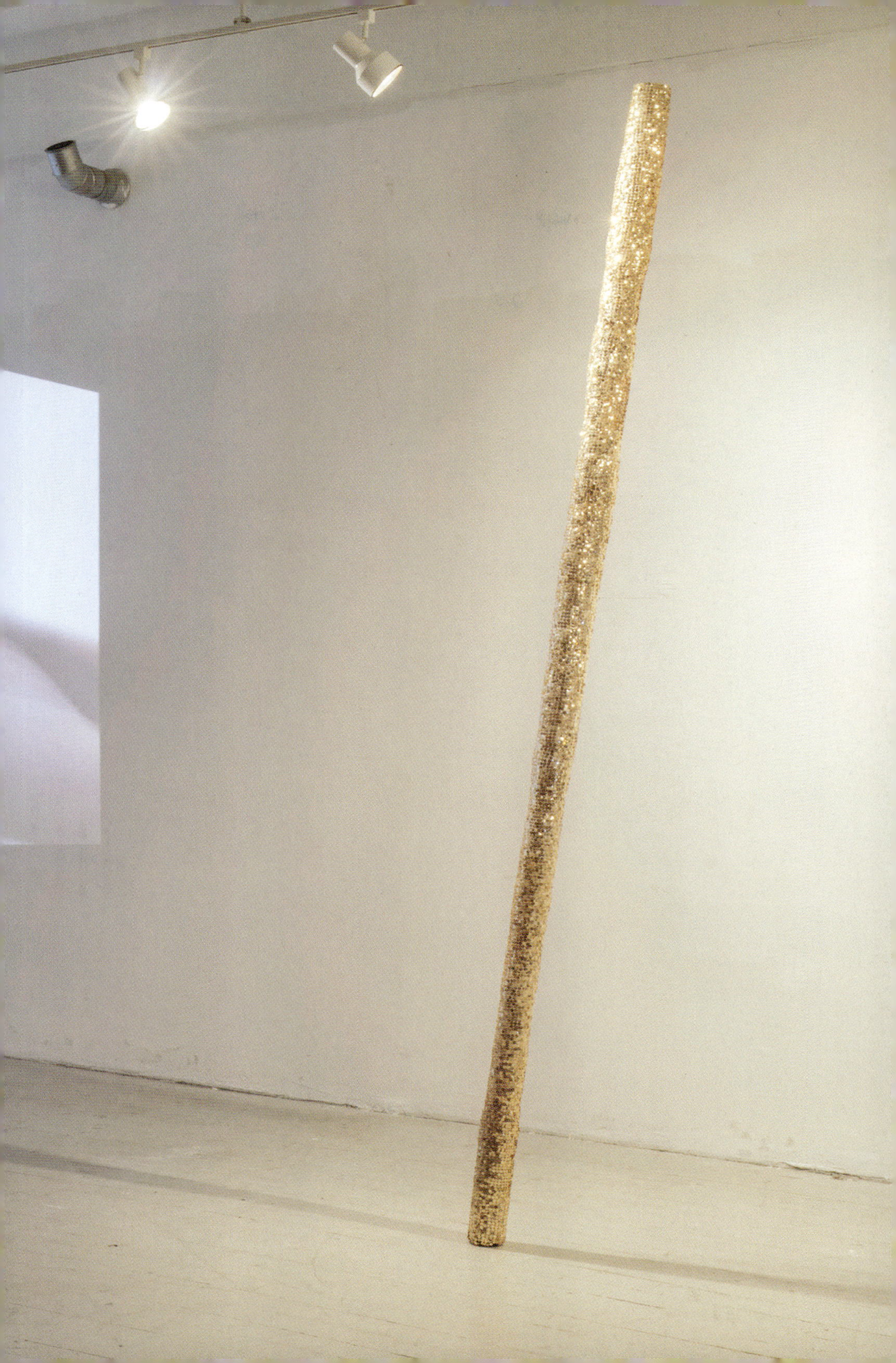

Notes on Visual Art

page

2   *D-lab*
Nickel Chromed Steel, Copper Plating, Parts from a Hard
Drive, Lamp Component
12 x 30 x 42 in
2013

4   *Tycoon*
20,000 Matchsticks, Hot Glue
120 x 72 x 48 in
2014

9-10   *Torpedo's*
Pool Noodles, Trash Can Lid, Matchsticks, Toothpicks,
Mylar, Roofing Cone
18 x 14 x 36 in
2012

17-18   *Table of the Sun*
Polyethylene Foam, Found Hardware, Magazine Clippings,
String, etc.
48 x 84 in
2013

22   *Tetra*
Polyethylene Foam, Found Objects
30 x 30 in
2013

24,   *Sforzinda*
29-30   Polyethylene, Found Hardware, Recycled Materials, String
etc.
48 x 84 in
2013

34,   *Pop*
84-85 Single Channel Video
       Video length 46:41
       Popping took 5 hours to get through 75 ft. of bubble wrap
       while popping each individual bubble.
       2015

54   *Glitch*
       Voice of Hal from 2001 Space Odyssey, Copper Plate,
       Etching Solution, Windshield-Wiper Motor, DC motor,
       Sponge, mdf, Arduino Components, Infrared Sensor, Alu-
       minium, Salt 4x4's, 8 ohm Speaker, Plywood, mdf
       2014
       Piece interacts with the audience via proximity sensor to
       trigger the movement of the wiper

58   *Ouroboros*
       Wood, Vinyl, Cats Meow Toy, Ink Transfer, Mac Screen
       Saver Projection
       30in diameter
       2014

64   *Morph*
       Polyethylene Foam, Forks, Tile Spacers, Q-tips, Paper, etc.
       30 x 30 in
       2012

66   *Plethora*
       120 x 204 in
       A duration-based collaborative installation over the course
       of two weeks using modular strategy of growth and perfor-
       mance meditation

       2013

70,
84-85   *Untitled*
        Steel, Sequins, Pins, Foam
        3 x 120 in
        2015
77

        Minecraft
        Polyethylene Foam, Carpet Foam, Q-tips, Magazine Clip-
        pings, Matchsticks, String, Wiggle Eyes, Paper, Electronic
        Cables, Straws
        21 x 12 in
        2013

About the Author

William Hicks is a poet from Kennesaw, Georgia. His work includes both digital
and print-based poetry, with a significant focus on the role of visual elements in
literary art. His digital work has been presented in numerous forums including
the 2012 Interrupt II Conference, the 2012 NEASA Digital Revolutions Con-
ference, and the 2014 Electronic Literature Organization Conference. His print
work appeared most recently in Synecdoche Magazine. He earned a master's
degree in physics in 2014 and is currently pursuing an MFA in poetry at Brown
University.

About the Artist

Maggie Hazen is a sculptor working with objects and multi-media used to
investigate alternative space existing parallel to normal everyday happenings.
She uses digital imagery alongside both kinetic and inert forms revolving around
perceptions of reality through science fiction and myth-making. She is a current
MFA candidate at the Rhode Island School of Design and received her BFA in
sculpture from Biola University. She has been presented in exhibitions interna-
tionally including the Los Angeles Museum of Tolerance and has participated
in numerous lectures and discussions on the topics explored in her work and
has been featured in a range of magazines and journals. She is featured in a
full-length documentary LAR-20 presented at the 6th Annual Korean American
Film Festival in New York.

About the Publisher

Synecdoche is a national literary arts journal and small press based in Providence, Rhode Island. Our publications are printed in Michigan and have a print run of 1,000. For more information, go to www.synecdochemagazine.com